HIM

HIMALAYA POEMS

KO UN

TRANSLATED BY
BROTHER ANTHONY OF TAIZÉ
AND LEE SANG-WHA

For Barbara & George
with my love
Anthony

GREEN INTEGER
KØBENHAVN & LOS ANGELES
2011

GREEN INTEGER
Edited by Per Bregne
København / Los Angeles
Distributed in the United States by Consortium Book
Sales and Distribution/Perseus
Distributed in England and throughout Europe by
Turnaround Publisher Services
Unit 3, Olympia Trading Estate
Coburg Road, Wood Green, London N22 6TZ
44 (0)20 88293009
ON NET available through Green Integer
(323) 857-1115 / http://www.greeninteger.com

Green Integer
6022 Wilshire Boulevard, Suite 202C
Los Angeles, California 90036 USA

First Green Integer Edition 2011
Korean edition published in 2000
Copyright ©2000 by Ko Un
Published in English by permission of the author.
English language translation ©2011 by
Brother Anthony of Taizé and Lee Sang-Wha
Back cover material ©2011 by Green Integer
All rights reserved

The publication of this book was supported by a generous grant
from the Korea Literature Translation Institute, Seoul, Korea

Series Design: Per Bregne
Book Design and Typography: Pablo Capra
Cover photograph: Ko Un

LIBRARY OF CONGRESS IN PUBLICATION DATA
Ko Un [1932]
Himalaya Poems
ISBN: 978-1-55713-412-7
p. cm – Green Integer 192
I. Title II. Series III. Translators: Brother Anthony and Lee Sang-Wha
Green Integer books are published for Douglas Messerli
Printed in the United States of America on acid-free paper.

In 1997, Ko Un and a few companions spent 40 days traveling rough through Tibet. He had learned some years earlier that one of his lungs had been rendered useless by an undiagnosed attack of tuberculosis in his youth. Notwithstanding that, he went walking over some of Tibet's highest passes, nearly dying of altitude sickness. While he was in Tibet, his mother died in Korea, although the news only reached him at the end of his journey. He was so affected by the lack of oxygen that after his return he could not write anything for a year or more. He finally recovered and composed this collection as a record of his Tibetan journey. It was published in the year 2000.

The translations have been revised in the light of numerous very helpful comments and suggestions made by Hillel Schwartz during a close reading of the draft text. The translators are most grateful to him for his labors.

The following five poems were first published in *Songs For Tomorrow* (Green Integer, 2009), in slightly different renditions: "Tibetan Night," "Name," "Sky Burial," "Mount Sumi," and "Optical Illusion."

CONTENTS

The Poet's Preface

With no hidden news in my heart, I crossed rivers. I struggled to climb up cliff after cliff. On many occasions I took the nearby mountains as my body and the far-away mountains as my neighbors.

Khora!

That was all the time with me. It meant turning, turning and turning, leaving the home of illusions and being worn out completely. However, the task of summoning up all the figures of this world's affairs and giving them names with an exhausted soul is always fresh.

In July 1997, I went to Tibet as if I was being kidnapped. I took it as a follow-up to the journey I had made through Nepal and India a few years before.

As we followed the Himalayas, at 6,500 meters I hung between life and death for lack of oxygen. Without proper treatment, I lost almost ten kilograms.

That forty days' journey to the North of the Himalayas was a bitter experience, well matching my reckless foolishness.

But I had something to say quietly : I went there, not in order to sing about the Himalayas but to sing about this world.

I believe that being far from the truth is poetic

truth. I do not say that just as a childish paradox.

No bird goes flying haphazardly. Although there is no trap in the sky to catch its wings no matter where it flies, there is clearly a path for birds to follow in the infinite sky. Even among the deepest mountain ranges under the sky there is a passage for birds and every kind of animal has its own secret passage.

Maybe men learned it from living creatures in nature; since ancient times humans have come to have their own passages. Perhaps I left because there exists such a path for me too. The path was endless, heading to the place where yesterday, today, eternally, the westerly wind comes from.

On reflexion, what has raised me is not the truth but the road. Who speaks the truth? The moment the truth is spoken it is spoiled. Whoever testifies to the truth distorts it. When the truth is given a name, systematized, and separated off into a sect, it is suffocated. Anyone who shouts that people should believe the truth is burying it. There is a saying, "You have only to open your mouth to meet with failure."

Then what Road, what Tao, should I speak of anew? How could I say that I seek the Tao where none exists?

All I hoped for was the buoyant heart I had in

my twenties. I just set off bearing that heart. The Sanskrit word "marga" means the passageway that enables one to reach a goal. I will call that passageway the Tao. Since there is no reason there should not be a goal for me, I was a traveler along the path. It was truly a long, long road along which I kept running, having nothing more to want. Several thousand kilometers of mortification made it possible for me to encounter that road.

I entered the continent's indifference with a traveler's melancholy on the far ranging Silk Road. That was also a fulfillment of my earnest prayer to encounter the hinterlands of history. Thinking of the ascetic monks of ancient times, who would walk five or ten kilometers every day along barren paths, I made them the genes of my pilgrimage. All that remained was the substance of a steadfast solitude from which sorrow and suchlike had all been banished. I passed along a long, rough road, something like the path to Hades, composed of rocks and wind, I passed Dunhuang's nights, and passed the never-ending plateau.

The Himalayas stretch for a length of 2,400 kilometers; their name is composed of two Sanskrit words, 'hima' (snow) and 'alaya' (dwelling). With Assam, Buthan, Sikhim to the East, Tibet to the North, Nepal, India, Pakistan to the South, the

Himalayas extend without ever coming to an end. Mountains rising over eight thousand meters, such as Everest, Lhotse, Makalu, Dhaulagiri, Manasulu, Anapurna peaks 1 and 2, paralleled my course at about half that altitude. I pursued my pilgrimage with those show-capped peaks in the distance one after another.

Finally, the majestic face of Nanga Parbat, on the Indian border, appeared in the sky, raising snowstorms. I stopped. It was in just these Himalayas that Asians' infinite cosmology, or inner cosmology, was born. That is why Mount Sumeru, in the midst of the Himalayas, is both a true mountain and a metaphysical mountain.

Mount Sumeru rises at a spot corresponding to the world's 'dantian' (lower abdomen). Beyond the Himalayas, it is venerated as a sacred mountain by Hindus, Buddhists and Jains. It is considered a mountain within the heart by all the schools of Tibet's native Bon religion and Lamaism, and even in the lands to the West along the Silk Road and the remote parts of China. As if realizing what the Katha Upanishad says, "Whatever is here, that is there; whatever is there, that is here," the Himalayas unite the worlds to their southern and northern sides.

Narrowly avoiding falls, I scrambled up and down precipices, crossed plains, on the way to the last place we could go. Now there seemed to be nowhere left for us to go, and nowhere for us to go back to.

When I wearily went outside after lying groaning in the tent, the stars filling the sky were intensely bright. My eyes grew brighter, my teeth tingled, my lungs trembled a lot. We were in regions at six thousand meters' altitude and you could feel, at heart, as though we were at six hundred thousand meters' altitude, so close to the stars. It is said you can see three thousand stars with the naked eye from the summit of Seorak-san mountain in Korea; from halfway up the Himalayas, nine thousand are said to be visible. Who could count them one by one! Even with the centrifugal force between just a single star and me, the distance is already eternal.

From the harsh road round the Changtang plateau, that means one whole tour of Tibet, I took my leave of the Himalayas. Then, on the plains to the North of the Himalayas, I was amazed to encounter cranes. They were embodiments of poetry.

The slope to the South of Dhaulagiri Peak is where the thirty-year-old Siddhartha went to seek out a teacher of truth. However, on a ridge of the northern slopes, rather than the southern, I was dreaming, not of freedom but of an unbounded freedom where even truth had been cast aside. Why, even truth can sometimes be a lack of freedom!

While I was wandering along the Silk Road my mother passed away. I only learned the news when I returned to Lhasa after going through all those hardships. Remorse that I had not been present at her death was the end of my pilgrimage to the Himalayas.

Three years later I started writing poems about my journey to the Himalayas.

After the Himalayas

It was not sorrow.
There were dazzling days
when I longed to tear out my eyes
and replace them with other eyes.
I came back from the Himalayas.
A child asked
what and what was there.
I longed to become the child's high voice.

—Ko Un

Himalaya Poems

Your Pilgrimage

A slower pace, a somewhat slower pace will do.
Of a sudden, should it start to rain,
let yourself get soaked.
An old friend, the rain.

One thing alone is beautiful: setting off.
The world's too vast
to live in a single place,
or three or four.

Walk on and on
until the sun sets,
with your old accomplice,
shadow, late as ever.
If the day clouds over,
go on anyway
regardless.

The Himalayas

Recollection is short, fantasy long!
A place where I'd never been born
and must never be born—
the Himalayas.

On whose behalf
did I go there?
I went with all ten fingers trembling.

With so many kinds of foolishness left back home,
I gazed up toward a few peaks
brilliant at eight thousand meters, their golden
    blades piled high.
Before that, and after,
I could not help but be an orphan.

I had but one hope:
to stay as far from the Himalayas as humanly
    possible,
and from the world of troublesome questions.
Yes, that was it.

That Name

After the year 1052,
throughout the highlands of the north,
in the gorges,
on the slopes and perilous cliffs
beneath perpetual snowfields,
all there was was
the name Milarepa.

For nearly one thousand years, that name was all
　　　there was.
After he passed away at the age of eighty-three.

Why, already in his lifetime,
the songs of the enlightened one,
his hundred thousand songs,
were all that existed
beyond this village
and that
and the mountain beyond.

After he died, as time flew like the sound of a flute
he was all there was that lived on,
far and wide across the Tibetan plateau.
All.

Note: Milarepa (1052-1135) is one of the most famous

figures in Tibetan history. In his youth he had been a magician, but having seen the futility of that, he spent years as a cave-dwelling hermit, to atone for the mayhem he committed to avenge wrongs done to his mother and sister, until he achieved enlightenment. He expressed that in the thousands of poems and songs he composed, many of which Tibetans know by heart.

Himalayan Slopes

Acknowledge the breathless time
in which that mountain
of ancient perpetual snow
and fresh coverlets of snow
lets itself melt over and over like a woman yielding
   her body.
Around three in the afternoon.

Around five
the meltwater rushes down, all at once.

If you can't escape in time
from the mad release,
then stay put,
telling yourself it would be good, too, to be swept
   on down.

Cross one river,
there's another.
Toss a stone,
what do you learn of water but depth?

From upstream a dead shepherd and two sheep
   come floating down.
Always and ever,
death here is nothing special.
While they were alive,

they were simply cold to the bone.

My one self became ten or twenty selves,
none of us able to move.
Here
there's no funeral
when you die.

Out of a surprisingly clear, open sky
a single drop of rain
whacked my brow.

A Village 4,300 Meters
Above Sea Level

Suddenly, a downpour.
Anyone walking just walks on.
Babies strapped on backs just get wet.
Everyone just gets wet.

No weather forecasts here,
no one asking wise women to guess at the weather.
Even the insects get wet when it rains;
once the rain stops they move on slowly over the
    wet ground.
It's been a long while
since they gave up on their dribbled guesses.

I'm thrilled that wisdom is so useless.

Darchen, Tibet —
a place obliged to become a street.
No umbrellas for the past thousand years.
People just walk along getting wet in the rain.
Once the rain stops their clothes dry. Slowly.
I asked:
Do you know Lhasa?
Have you been to Lhasa?
He answered:
I don't know.

A not-knowing happiness, theirs,
a not-knowing nirvana,
a life day by day, not-knowing.

The Peak Next to Dhaulagiri

Dear!
You've come as a departed spirit,
your empty body left behind.
Fifteen or sixteen days after your demise
you've reached this distant place.

The road leading to the town of Ali
had been nothing but empty mountains, empty
    slopes—
all so utterly empty
nothing could survive
or settle anywhere.

A place bordering India, Nepal, Kashmir:
the netherworld west of Tibet.

A place where the long arc of the Himalayas folds
    its wings
and meets the spine of the Gangdis Range,
the spine of the Karakoram;
a place where the Kunlun Mountains hunker
    down.

That place,
often called the roof of the world,
was utterly empty.

People live here.
It's not the world beyond,
it's this world,
and I'm alive in it,
eating a skewerful of mutton
a young Uighur has cooked for me.

Wilderness

A wilderness 5000 meters up.
Oblivious of father
or mother,
I
stand alone here.

And completely devoid of green.

By green I mean
the memory of all the green I've ever seen.

Come racing, wild beasts,
race up
and claw at my gaunt body.
Gnaw it.

Fear and pain coincident--
in the aftermath
peace and wilderness
would no longer be distinct.
Despair is the honey of despair.

Tale of Lhasa

In ancient times,
contemplating the future of his kingdom,
King Songchen Gompo, lord of united Tibet,
sent twenty of the brightest youths
from across the Himalayas
down to India to the university at Naranda.
Over the course of several years
they studied philosophy, mathematics, astronomy.
Seventeen of the twenty died of chronic diseases.
The remaining three
came back to Tibet.
But two of them died soon after their return;
one survived in dimwitted dementia.

To the people of Lhasa over 3000 meters up,
the world down below was like the world of the
    dead.
On the other hand,
youths from China's Sichuan province
who came recklessly up to Tibet
could not survive in a world 3700 meters above sea
    level.
They too died one after another.

Yet now the Sichuanese in Lhasa's new suburbs
are becoming Tibet's ruling elite,
living well, prospering.

The Tibetan people
are becoming hoarse, penniless tramps,
what with strong Chinese liquor and syphilitic
sluts.

A Baby

Someone measured Namjagbarwa peak
in the Nyainqentanglha range in eastern Tibet
and found it to be 7756 meters high.

Beyond that peak,
beyond mountains
and more mountains
lies a village, Jinuk,
a shantytown of twelve families.

On the brown slopes overlooking Jinuk
is a tattered tent.
A woman lives there who once was known as
    Tsringanmo,
but she has no need for a name now.
She kneads dough outside the tent.

She went into labor.
You see, she was at term.
"I'll come back after giving birth,"
she said.
She stopped kneading
and went into one corner of the tent,
screening herself vaguely with a remnant of cloth.
Very soon she gave birth to the baby.
Holding on to the tent
she gave birth standing up.

She gave birth smoothly.

The baby, laid in a basket,
was already making its first weak cries.

Then the woman came back out.
Complaining that the dough had hardened a little,
she added more water.

It was like a hen laying an egg,
like a horse dumping a load.
The intensely blue sky was blinking its eyes.

A year later the baby was given its name,
the commonest of names, Tensing.
His grandfather had also been named Tensing.

One Night on the High Plateaux

Scorpions
mites
midges
mosquitoes were themselves night;
mosquitoes
flies
gadflies that bore into a cow's hide were the day.

Outside the tent
people wore hats with gauze veils.
Inside
they hung plastic bags filled with water.

When I go back, shall I exaggerate,
claiming I was greatly enlightened overnight?

Seagulls

Over the Changtang plateau
the Tibetan gulls were flying
at an altitude above 5000 meters
near the northern face of the Himalayas.

A long time ago,
a million years back,
this region was a sea.
Then, roaring and booming,
the roof of the world came surging up.

Never able to make it back to the sea
the gulls have survived on this plateau
generation after generation.

Now they don't know the whereabouts of the
    Indian Ocean.
Don't know the whereabouts of any sea.
On the peak of Kangchendzonga in morning's
    golden sun
they were alighting
and gazing with bright eyes
on outcroppings clearly within range,
not those impossibly remote.

A Family of Five Generations

At the foot of the slopes of a mountain of black
    rock,
totally black rock,
there's a hidden meadow.
Without fail
a nomad's tent is pegged-down there,
and a flock of sheep grazes.

Great-great-grandfather
great-grandfather
grandfather, grandmother
father
mother
the youngest son, six-year-old Tensing.

Tensing came running:
"Grandpa,
a lamb's been born."

At that
great-grandfather
and grandfather together responded:
"Ah, yes?"
"Ah, yes?"

Great-great-grandfather
and great-grandfather

and grandfather too
were all "Grandpa."

Great-great-grandfather however
was deaf
so couldn't gather that a lamb had been born
and thought Tensing was just saying he'd come
     home:
"Ah, yes?"

Great-grandfather's 72
grandfather's 53
father's 32
Tensing's 6
nobody knows how old great-great-grandfather is
maybe 89 or 90;
he himself has no idea.

The sheep came home by themselves,
one hundred seventy of them.
Two days ago one died,
today one was born.

On the other side of the mountain,
Tensing's two older brothers, twelve-year-old twins,
were tending the flock of another shepherd.
The brothers gazed up with their naked eyes
at the nine thousand stars in the night sky.
The starlight, the starlight

that had fallen into the sleeping eyes of the five
    generations
fell asleep there.
Tomorrow they must look for other pastures,
meadows that lie flat,
so difficult to find.

Strange to tell,
it's great-great-grandfather
and the ewes who find the meadows first.

Pointing: "That way . . ."

More Than Once

The cry of a newborn, still bloody.
It's not a baby on my back
but Annapurna,
rising behind me.

Tomorrow and the next day too, it is a blessing
not to know at all than to know too well.

It's not just Annapurna.
Everything
arises more than once.

I walked on, limping,
into the multiple lives of a flower.
Eddies carried swiftly down the rapids
echoed below, weeping and alone.

I long faintly for the outside world,
all of it a distant memory.

Stories

There are stories.
There are people telling stories
and people listening to them.

The room is full
of the breath of the stories.

That is enough.

Eight months of winter at minus 40.
A weaned baby froze to death;
the grieving did not last long.

Soon there are stories.
Between prayers and more prayers
between one meal and the next
there are stories.
This kind of state is perfect.

An Empty Can

A set of spare clothing, patched,
and a blanket
Phaaw!
What a stench.
A bag of barley flour
some rock salt
tea
dried fruit
a water pot
a recently acquired empty can.

Those suffice for months on a mountain slope.

Tents ten or fifteen kilometers away
the nearest neighbors.

They set fire to dried dung
warm their faces
and go to sleep around ten p.m.
The sun doesn't set till then.
Starlight erupts in unison
and the darkness beams through, here and there.

They never realize that this is poverty.
On rainy days it's not easy to strike fire from a
     flint.

A Spring in a Cave

Rinpoche entered a cave.
His companion
walled up the cave from the outside.

All was darkness,
all that remained were prayers.

Once a day tea and tsampa were passed into the
    cave.

That went on for twelve years.
For thirty years.

There was no time inside.
A friend came visiting.
That friend was Death.

Ten years after he died
the friend who had left him came back and opened
    the cave.
There were bones,
and under the bones spring water was rising.

Children

Tibetan children,
their stiff hair heavy with dust,
call their fathers dad.
They call men of their father's age dad too.
Rightly so,
rightly so.
How could my birth-father be my only father?
Men of my father's age
are other kids' dads
and so aren't they my dad too, when I'm of their
    age?

Deep in the mountain shade
in the air
beyond the hot sunlight
glow the whites of the eyes of children
who are growing up well
though they have no clothes.

The air is their dad as well.

Calming the Breath

Poised like an ageing bear
climbing a tree, hanging on tightly,
I collect my breath.

Poised like a bird
stretching its neck out and pecking at food
I collect my breath.

Heaven and earth are full of breath.
When a dragon chants, a cloud rises.
When a tiger whistles in reply,
it becomes the wind.

While breath moves in and out in this way,
the breath grows calm
the breath grows calm.

From the foot of Mount Kunlun onward
I grew miserly with breathing.
Exhale, inhale,
calming the breath.

The Blind Man of Mount Sumeru

One complete circuit of Mount Sumeru
takes two days
or three.

If you make a full prostration at every step,
one complete circuit
takes a month
or more.

On the west side of Mount Sumeru
at the foot of a cliff a thousand leagues high
a withered blind man was sitting.

I did not address him,
I addressed the rock he was seated on.

Gazing up at Mount Sumeru
gazing up at that sacred mountain
year after year
he'd been gradually blinded by its dazzling
    brightness
until now, he said, he could see nothing.

So now, he said, he saw with his heart,
he saw with the eyes of his heart.

He laughed

in that utter darkness.
That laugh
with the few yellow teeth he still had left
was a happiness beyond all happiness.

My companion and I walked on.

Note: Mount Sumeru (Meru), a mythical mountain in Buddhist cosmology, is also an alternative name for Mount Kailas.

Hope

It was during the four months when the low
     grasses grew.
It was the time when, once they had grown,
seeds like weeping eyes
ripened.
I fell, again and again.

The flowers blossoming in my eyes
quickly bloomed and
as quickly withered.
Then seeds formed and ripened.

After eating a handful of rye-barley flour
I drank some water.
I walked on once more.

Ahead of me a person said:
There is hope.
Another person asked:
What is hope?
I shook my head.
No one
had spoken to me.
It was a phantom.
There was nothing following me
but a dog so old it could not bark.
I tossed the creature the scrap of bread I had left.
It didn't even wag its tail.

Tibetan Night

Several floors
above any other night on earth
there was the Tibetan night.
For a long time.

That is, at least ten times ten thousand years.

In the dark, fully fermented,
darknesses became wine.

Next morning, as the sunlight
glinted over icy rocks 8000 meters up,
here,
there,
the lingering dead-drunk darkness
awoke the night over nomads' tents.

Odd.
Tibet has no need of religion
yet it's nothing but religion.
Om Mani Padme Hum.
It has no need of stray dogs,
yet stray dogs roam across its plains.
Om Mani Padme Hum.

Note: *Om Mani Padme Hum* is a Sanksrit formula

meaning, literally, "Om, jewel in the lotus, hum" ("Om" and "hum" being "seed syllables"). The oldest and perhaps most important mantra of Tibetan Buddhism (in Tibetan 'om mani peme hung'), there is a range of explanations and levels of interpretation. The jewel can represent the mind of enlightenment which arises in the lotus of human consciousness, for example.

Snowman

The north face of Manasulu, 8000 meters high,
is a black cliff rising. Perpendicular.
A perpendicular
more than perpendicular.
It must pour wantonly down.
It must collapse.

Beyond
that black north face
are snowfields so old
we cannot bear to look at them.

There, there are footprints,
the Snowman's footprints.

Neither man's nor beast's,
there are footprints
whose plodding can be heard.
Surrender.
If you stare up,
it's already all golden light.

It's white at first,
all so white
that the eyes grow sick.
Now it all looks golden.

You don't need things like the Snowman's
	footprints.
Returning to this world,
you don't need all the world's curses.
Back home, you should be mute for the rest of
	your life.

A Stream

It was quite unexpected.
At the foot of the soaring, winding Tangkura
    Ridge,
there, too,
a village.
No matter if some sing of it as paradise.
No matter if others call them animals.

Pitiful, the stream that flows before the few houses.
At times it dries up completely;
at times,
after rain has fallen,
it flows to its own tune.

On a day like that
two women are doing washing, for the first time in
    years;
they do not let the dirty water run back into the
    stream
but empty it into the far fields
so that folks further down will have clean water.

In Tibet, washing is done only once every several
    years.
Five years,
maybe seven.
Babies have no diapers,

and once the rag soaked with shit has dried
it's used again
until a large rag has grown very small.

In the long run, after a burst of laughter, there's a
    future life.

Buddhas Embracing

The interlaced Buddhas
slipped in stealthily one dark night.

Buddha
and his wife
or his lover
are embracing tightly.
Uhuhuhuhuhuh,
Tantric Yoga,
the panting prior to orgasm.

What wretch would dare interrupt them?
They are in perfect Samadhi.
If some wretch should force his way in,
the outer heavens would be wrathful
and the underworld infuriated to its depths.

Ah! the climax!
A prayer to them at that moment is the most
    sacred,
a hundred times more sacred
than a prayer to Shakyamuni Buddha
or Amitabha Buddha sitting, exhausted from work,
merely dignified, benign.

A Remote Village

Flutter to your heart's content,
faded prayer flags!
Once we'd passed Chanche
we saw them again
in a place where they were not supposed to be,
in a village
in the wind
where a few black curs, never barking,
treat master and guest alike.

The village is large or small
according to the quantity of water
flowing down the mountains from the melting
    snow and ice.

When the sun sets at 10:00 pm
and ancient, naive darkness falls,
there's no lamplight.
At night, everything's dark.
Once night's past
day's sure to come.
I cried out in a loud voice.
The sound sped off
then vanished, unable to make up even half the
    distance.

The mountains are vast

the plains are vast
the villages grow ever smaller until they disappear.
The large crows aloft
look to be vigorous.
Waiting for someone to die,
waiting to devour the carrion
once someone has died,
they make dignified circles in the air, not the least
    bit impatient.

Good.

Light

The world was all aglimmer.
Utterly impossible
for one woman
to love one man;
for one man
to love then hate one woman.
It was all aglimmer.

Knowledge decomposed,
lost in ignorance.
Far off mountains were very close.

I was standing there, at the end of the West
    Changtang Plateau.
I cast no shadow.
Even shadows,
shadows themselves were all light.

Deep into the night, stars were pouring down
torrents of starlight,
and all was aglimmer.
Even my entrails were visible, squirming.

The sky above the central Himalayas,
the blizzards
and the clouds--

all aglimmer with light.
Graceful as a spy,
a glimmer of light slipped in close beside me.

Amitabha on Horseback

It was a dizzying wonder, in which a lie
turned in secret to truth.
A cloudless day, hundreds of miles around,
and so cold it made one shiver head to toe.

A rashness like the charge of a wild boar!
This day was a desert,
all such astonishments gone.

A mummy buried in the middle of the desert
emerged.
And with it
a statue of Amitabha on horseback
elaborately sculpted
during the Northern Wei Dynasty.

Leaving the mummy out of it,
just look at this guy.
Look at this guy.
Amitabha in stone, out for a ride.

We should have drunk together
with this Amitabha today,
tomorrow with his sister,
or with his wife.

There was a leave-taking as he departed on

     horseback,
a leave-taking as his sister and wife saw him off.
The desert
buries all such leave-takings
and covers them with a blanket of windborne
     sand.

You who set off for the west:
I pray that you live on,
be it as a scorpion
or an idiot who knows nothing of right or wrong.

Left Alone

They have set off in search of a man who went
    astray,
lost in a perilous ravine.
Alone
I remain in the tent.
How hosts of past cowardices
become my friends!

Here
like this
like this
be solitary just for ten years.

I shall turn into something
different.
My left side will become
my right side.

On the third night
there was still no sign
of the lost man or of those who'd gone searching.
In a ravine near China's Jinghai salt flats,
still remembering who I was
I roared like a wild animal.

About a Child

It was a highland village,
a village
we had really struggled to reach,
breathless all the way.

The name of the village doesn't really matter.
Could be Murji, or not.

A name's really
a sixth finger
stuck on to the usual five.

A five-year old child in that village, a six-fingered
    child,
has been leading a really hard life
from the moment he was born in this world.

He would carry firewood
all day long, until sunset,
not knowing how to cry.
His night was long with darkness,
not really knowing how to caress.

Oasis

Nothing but the color green
and the sound of weeping.
I wish
it could be like this
on the day the world ends.

Still, this world here below
is more inclined to have no compassion
than to have compassion.
Far more.

His life ended with a gulp of oasis water.
I closed my dead friend's open eyes.

Meeting a Downpour

I'll give you everything!

We were on the Changtang Plateau.
Pitch dark on all sides.
Thunder. Lightning.
And rain poured down.
Not one of the many gods, anywhere.
Not one of so many memories.
It was dark.

Over my head lightning cleft the air.
Rrrrr KWANG
and again: Rrrrr KWANG.

I could not take a single step.
My body trembled so hard that I fell gravely ill.

The Third Dalai Lama

Ha! ha ha!
In 1587, the Drepung monastery outside Lhasa
    was magnificent.
Lamas in yellow hats
filled the courtyard of the monastery.
There the venerable Sonam Gyatso
received the title of Dalai Lama
from Altan Khan, King of Mongolia.

The sound of drums filled the air,
and long drawn out flutes.

He was the first Dalai Lama.

But he believed there'd been two Dalai Lamas
    before him
and today he was succeeding those.

Not only in waking hours
but also in his dreams
he saw himself as he had been in the past
the first Dalai Lama,
and the second.

So he called himself the third Dalai Lama,
not the first.

I was before.
I am the I before me
and the I after.

I am all their many pasts.
I am all their many tomorrows, too.
A few years ago
I met the 14th Dalai Lama.
I asked him:

"Who are you?"
His knees shaking, he laughed:
"I don't know. It's been such a long time . . . ."

The Sixth Dalai Lama

He enjoyed debauchery.
enjoyed drinking,
enjoyed women.
Flesh, yes!
Flesh!

Days of grand religious ceremony irritated him
    most.
All such rituals were mere lies.

Perhaps the seventh Dalai Lama
was an aftermath of self-indulgence
in a previous life:
an idiot
echoing a dummy.

He cared for nothing.
Thought of nothing.
He just liked windy days, this way or that.

At last,
Tibet fell under the control of the Ch'ing.
Prayer flags fluttered in the wind very, very idly.

The Dalai Lama's Younger Brother

He died when he was two.
The grief was half-hearted.

An astrologer said:
Don't bury him.
Let him lie.
He'll come back to life . . . so just leave him there.

They put a butter stain on the corpse.

That selfsame stain was found on the body
of a child born the following year.

So the little brother of the 14th Dalai Lama
grew up happily as the son of another couple.
That family's flock of sheep increased threefold.

The young shepherd was good at driving them.
He was good at milking them, too.
His elder brother in a previous life
is renowned in Daramsala and in New York
while he lives nameless
among the Tibetans of Changtu in China
He's 62 or 63 this year.
He's forgotten how old.

Old Clothes

That day each year when the Dalai Lama
left the Potala for the summer palace of Nobrinka
was the day when Tibetans changed their clothes.

It was not a country for washing clothes.

They lived with smells of yak, goat, pig.
Once they gone any distance in new clothes
they had hardly begun to speak when they had the
      same stench.
Tibet's animals
and Tibet's people were not two.
The prayer flags
and the wind were not two.
The wind blew that smell away particle by particle.
That's how the wind asks, and answers.

Phowa

I want to leave this world just about now.
I have no reason to go on living.
Phowa.
It's a way of putting an end to one's life.
Phowa.

I'll die tomorrow.

One day later
he stopped breathing and died
as he said he would.

No struggling
to stay alive to the end,
to the very end, which anyhow doesn't exist:
just stopping his breath,
inviting death.
There is a dignity to this, a kind of human dignity.

Note: *Phowa*, or "transference of consciousness at the time of death," is the Tibetan Buddhist method for ensuring that one attains enlightenment after the present life ends. Through a combination of breath, mantra, and visualization techniques exercised at the time of death, the consciousness departs through the crown of the head. From this gate one's consciousness can be transferred directly to the pureland of Buddha Amitabha or Dewachen.

Child as Teacher

Setting a child, tiny as a baby quail,
on the highest throne,

serving a thoughtless child
who knows nothing but the ease of crying,

bowing down on their knees
to a child
as their highest master,

that is the multiple hundredfold beauty of Tibetan
    Buddhism.

Ah,
let go of that five-thousand-year-old
antiquated art called beauty.

A Statue of 12-Year-Old Siddhartha

Jokhang Temple in Lhasa
was all bright colors, clouded with the smoke of
    incense.
There
a healthy man might limp
or fall down,
or tumble down foaming at the mouth
or grin broadly unawares.

Through corridors in darkness
butter-lamps flicker dully.
There are statues there that have been sitting for a
    thousand years.
Deep within
there's old Rinpoje, his mouth tight shut,
survivor of the cultural revolution.

Go crazy!
Go crazy!

There are mice there that live on the butter in the
    lamps,
mice without tails.
There are lamas there who catch those mice,
cure and sell them.
A stone Siddhartha, age twelve, has been sitting
    there

among the statues of buddhas and boddhisattvas
since ancient times.
I couldn't breathe.

I dashed out of there and ran wildly away.
The beggars followed me, then gave up.
I came alive thanks to the winds from the Yarlung
    Tsangpo River.

The current ran swiftly.
Here, in the river,
children twelve or thirteen years old were
    splashing.

Lake Rakshastal

Lake Manasarovar is a lake of light.
It's a lake where the forty Himalayan peaks,
peaks that rise more than 7000 meters,
stop at least once
on their way from east to west,
west to east.

It's a lake like the sea,
like a mirror reflecting all the seas.
It's a lake where the white peaks stop.
Vying with that lake is Lake Rakshastal,
its neighbor,
a lake of devils, where the peaks also stop.

All day long
there is nothing for Rakshastal to reflect
but the sky,
the clouds in the sky.
I plunged into that lake naked.
All the way in.
But in the time it took to climb out,
my body had dried in a flash.

It was a lake without so much as a breath of wind,
let alone devils.
The weakest of regrets were reflected in it, then
    disappeared.

Grandmother

She performed 1000 prostrations every day.
In the course of a 100-day prayer,
she made 100,000 prostrations.
The more ignorant, the more glorious is the
    prostration.
The more incapable, the more sincere is the prayer.
After those prayers
she quit the world.
The lice crept away unnoticed
from between her white hairs.
Crows ate her flesh,
insects ate what was left.
Her grandson made a necklace
with the scraps of her bones
and hung it around his dirty neck.

Leo Tolstoy's *On Life* was just a book.
I was completely helpless.

Sky Burial

The site, halfway up a mountain, was a mound of
    pebbles.
Among the pebbles
some stunted trees were growing.
A corpse lay stiff
across a flat rock.

The cutting was skillfully done.
The entrails were drawn out.
Then the young son, a surgeon,
cut open the heart and examined the parts.
The gall bladder and kidneys were examined too.

The head was removed.
The spine was taken out.
The ribs were stripped and piled separately.

The officiant went down the hill blowing a bone
    flute.
No sooner was he gone
than a large vulture descended from above,
furled its wings,
and began to gorge itself.
A bit later a big raven arrived
and ate its fill.

Other birds followed one by one.

The wind did not sit still;
rising, it swept fiercely across the mountainside.

Dialogue

Maybe peaks I and II of Annapurna
are half-brothers
rather than full-blood brothers.
Or perhaps
neither knows what the other is
even after such a long time together,
nor who their parents are.

They remain some sixty kilometers apart;
one is sometimes hidden by blizzards,
then suddenly becomes clear.
Without a single word,
they face each other's white faces
and talk as mutes do.

Let's sink down now.
Let's stop soaring.
Let's sink really deep down into the earth
where everything's dark
Let's.
Yes.

Kochi! Kochi!

Kochi! Kochi!
"You're really the best!"
That's what the beggars say in Octagon Street in
    Lhasa's old town.
Kochi! Kochi!

Much more splendid than, "Got a penny?"

You're the best!
You're really the best!

Holding up one grubby thumb:

Kochi! Kochi!

Hearing that, I felt great
so gave one a Chinese bank-note.
Surrounded by more beggars
unable to move, I started to sweat.
Kochi!
Kochi!
Kochi!
Kochi!

Abandoned Old Man

It was a slope 5000 meters up.
It was a wilderness with nothing,
nothing at all.

A tiny, tattered tent stood on the slope,
a tent handed down through four generations.
In it there was an old man.
He didn't know if his vacant eyes
could see or not.

The previous day his son and daughter-in-law
and his eight-year-old grandson
had made their last bows, falling to their knees.

In the tent, there was food,
a change of clothes,
a bundle of firewood to calm the cold.

He'd recovered a bit from the snow-blindness
he'd suffered a few years before
but was becoming increasingly deaf.
Now there was almost nothing he could see or
      hear.
So a few days later he'd just die.
The crows would come for him.
Eagles too would come flying in.
All the feathered creatures he'd lived with all those

80

        years
would see to his funeral rites.

He'd dreamed a dream the previous night:
how, as a child, he'd clapped his palms together
on seeing the run of ripples after a downpour.

Khora

Turning
Turning

Khora

The eye of the typhoon in the sky is turning.
The nucleus of matter is splitting and turning.

The Earth is turning.
The hands of the clock are turning.

In Tibetan Buddhism, they turn clockwise
in Bon they turn counterclockwise.

Khora

It takes three or four days to make one circuit
    around Mount Kailas
but two bored lamas
leave at dawn and
arrive back at the same place in Darchen that
    night.

Turning.
Turning.

This world is turning.
I am turning.

Mummies

Before the Taklamakan desert
comes the Lop desert,
where mummies appear and disappear.
As sand dunes vanish
in the blowing wind
ancient mummies appear.
As the wind rises and shapes new sand dunes
they are buried again.
A gaunt millennium has passed.

A Death

There's a mirror from Tsaparang Palace in Guge,
a kingdom that lasted two hundred years.
The people who should be
reflected in that mirror do not exist.
They died.

After dying,
even corpses' faces vanished.

Death is not a spiritless body left behind after the
    spirit has departed.
Both spirit and body have vanished.
An empty mirror is all there is.

The Eastern Himalayas

Makalu is 8475 meters high.
Lhotse, 8501 meters.
Chomolangma, 8848.
Nuptse, 7879.
Kangchendzonga, 8584.
Cho Oyu, 8153.

I saw those altitudes listed in a mud-walled hut
called the Everest Hotel.

After an evening's rest,
I stroked the heads of a dozen boy monks
at Rongbuk Monastery in Tingri
and gave them a photo of the Dalai Lama
that I had brought with me.

Other white mountains spread themselves out
across the sky,
fold after fold of mountain ranges
after crossing breathless Pangla Pass.
More peaks, not counting the forty
over 7000 meters high.
Let's go down.
Down, please.
Going up is no truth.

Shigatse

There lived the splendid Panchen Lama,
the equal of the Dalai Lama.
He died, amidst many doubts,
at Tashilhunpo Monastery
in Tibet's second city, Shigatse.

On the empty ground in front of the monastery,
look: dogs lying flat on their stomachs.
Caring little for the tedious bowing of all the
    women
falling to their knees,
the dogs just lie there, flat on their stomachs.

Outside Tashilhunpo, the wind wakes the sleeping
    dust.
Inside, old monks and child monks
live together without regard,
murmuring most admirably.

Optical Illusion

It's very close.
And very, very clear.
Over there.

Yet after a full day's journey
it's as far off as ever; unreachable.

Close-seeming far-off spot.

We need far-off people like that.
Very close by.

Sky-Burial Site at Dolma-la Pass

I did not ask him why he was making the circuit.
Following at a distance, I just made
one remote circuit.

It takes some people
one full day
to make the circuit around Mount Kailas
from left to right;
some people take three days.
Some take more than a month,
falling full-length with each step, bodies like
      inchworms.

Some make not one circuit
but ten circuits
one hundred circuits
one hundred eight circuits.

If someone happens to die circling
5600 meters up,
the place they drop becomes a platform
for a sky-burial.

Shreds of the clothes of the dead lie scattered
      there,
and abandoned shoes.

Shards of bone too, scattered and alone.

Not the false opal that melts in hot water,
the sky is honestly the deepest blue.

Inside the Potala

I lost track of my three companions.
In the dark labyrinth
I walked aimlessly, calling out for no one.
I had no idea where I might be.
I wandered on.

I kept sneezing.
Butter lamps flickered like palsied hands.
After thirty minutes
I was almost used to the wandering.

I bumped my head hard
against the pillar of an altar
for the mummy of one Dalai Lama.

Now I no longer wanted to meet up with any of
    my companions.
I wanted to wander on without them, alone,
until I found myself outside.
Forty minutes or so of solitude.
On the shady stairway outside the palace
there they were,
the other three.
Abruptly I turned away.
From now on, a new life.

A Long Night

We put up a tent for the night
between Shigatse and Latse.
As soon as the tent was up
a storm broke.
The tent shook as if about to fly away.

The water rose
up the river bank,
and with it the loud sound of the stream.

Shortly before, our water had boiled at 80
     Centigrade.
Not anything like 100.
My anxiety and resignation had boiled away with
     it.

Already unrecallable sights have been swept away.
The sound of the river rose louder still.
The only thing left for me was to be swept away in
     the swollen stream.
I recalled my wife's face.
I recalled my daughter's face.
I had absolutely no use for things like truth.

Landscape

Until now, I had painted the world with a few
    colors.
I had insisted that a few things in the world
were the whole of it.

The waters of the Yarlung Tsangpo River run
    swiftly;
we were drawn together.

The mountains looked like
someone had spent a lifetime making them
or, one lifetime proving insufficient,
several generations.
The mountains were perfect, solid bodies;
their slopes were precise straight lines
without the least superfluity.

Just for today I hate curves.

A child
was teasing his brain awake with snuff
at the spot where he had halted his flock.
His cloudy mind cleared,
he saw the green rape fields
on the brink of the world
far below.
It was too early for the rapeseed to blossom.

Nothing here to get drunk on but liquor.
We dispersed.

I despise the five colors of Tibet.
Somewhere beyond the Himalayas
one man gained enlightenment
and a five-hued radiance,
it's said,
spread out from his body.
Since then everything here has been stained with
     five colors.

Blue
White
Red
Green
Gold

Kumbum Monastery

It once had one hundred eight halls.
Kumbum Monastery
was Kumbum Monasteries.
What, so many?
You don't get it.
One hundred eight halls weren't enough.
Every day
all the mountains and plains
as well as the corridors between the halls
they were temple halls, too.

All the Buddhas' eyes in all the halls were flying
     eyes,
eyes flying as birds fly.

The birds were buddhas, I now realize.
Their songs were sutras,
their droppings relics of buddhas.
How tedious!
Better to end five thousand years of religion
now. . . .

Shangri-la

Like a kind of contradiction
it must exist in some valley in the great Himalayan
     range.
Where life is completely impossible,
somewhere here,
paradise has to exist, totally concealed.

In bitterest cold, fifty below,
somewhere here
must exist a paradise of perpetual springtime,
late springtime days,
a paradise of flowers and maidens,
of precious stones and simple, honest men.

Shangri-la!
It has to exist.
It is where my dearest friends have gone;
it must exist.

Shangri-la, our millennial temptation,
you have to be here.

A Life

A thousand years ago
a wealthy man lived in the remote village of Kya
    Ngatsa.
In his lands between the mountains
he tended a flock of six thousand sheep.
At home his son Thopaga was growing up,
and Thopaga's younger sister Peta.

As soon as Thopaga's father died,
his father's faithful cousins took possession of all:
house, land, buildings, animals.
The mother and two children became their serfs
and survived by eating scraps from their table.

The mother's heart was full of thoughts of her
    dead husband
and hatred for those who had stolen their
    inheritance.
Tortured by resentment
every night she would beat at the floor and walls.

When her son, nine on the day his father died,
    grew to be fifteen,
she made him master the ancient black arts--
death-dealing; raising storms.

He killed his uncle's and aunt's family,

Thirty-five, betrayers all.
Then he called down hail to flatten the village,
a disastrous hail destroying crops and animals.

Revenged, Thopaga left home.
For six years and seven months
he did penance deep inside the mountains
guided in ascetic practice by the monk Marpa.
In his cave he lived on chopped nettles
until his body grew green.

Meanwhile, his mother died
and his sister Peta went begging,
as did Zesay, the woman to whom he had been
        betrothed.

Thopaga became known as Milarepa.
One day that dark cave
filled with light.
His mind and the world had become fully one.
There was neither self nor other.

From that time
he went wandering through the world.
Everywhere he went
he comforted people,
drawing off a little of the darkness
from their heavy hearts.
He sang.

He sang.
The vast world,
lucent like a vast mirror,
followed after those songs
as they faded in the distance.

He was a singer until he was eighty-three.

One day, overflowing with joy,
Milarepa turned into water.

Unaware,
his disciple Rechungpa tossed a stone into the
    water.
The next day Milarepa returned into his body.
He said:
My breast is sore, for last night I was struck by a
    stone.
His disciple found a small stone there and drew it
    out.
Then the old master felt comfortable.
As if at recreation, he smiled brightly, then closed
    his eyes.

No one knows where his mummy is.
Maybe someone lifted
his skull and bones.

After his death

his songs were passed down.
Some vanished;
others still roam Tibet
as his Hundred Thousand Songs.

Farewell

She hung rayon *hadas*,
white scarves,
about my neck.
I was happy.
Utterly happy.

> Once you're back home,
> remember me now and then.

It was on a plateau more than 5000 meters up.
Blue poppies
were blooming in profusion
over the whole pebbled plateau
beyond an open-air sulfur spring.
By those flowers I would remember her;
she said:

> Be sure to remember me.

A tear flowed, even in that lofty realm.

Potala Palace

Despite the harsh poverty across Tibet's highlands
each inch of the Potala is crusted with gold, silver,
    and gems.
White Palace and Red Palace have nine hundred
    ninety-nine rooms
populated by a vast confusion
of wood and stone
buddhas
bodhisattvas
shrines of successive Dalai Lamas
brilliant murals.

Stone and wood
were dragged up tributaries of the Yarlung
    Tsangpo River.

Loads of juniper and cedar
were brought from Bhutan or somewhere
beyond the snowy mountains
to frame story after towering story.

In the seventh century,
Songtsen Gampo established a great kingdom in
    these highlands;
his forces pushed into China as far as Changan,
    capital of the T'ang.

Again, in 1642,
Tibet became once more a great kingdom.
Three years later
the fifth Dalai Lama began building the Potala.

Potalaka is the mythical home of the great
    bodhisattva
Avalokitesvara, guardian of the sea.
That name Potalaka
became Potala.
That legendary island in the vast cosmic ocean
became the Potala in Lhasa.

Four years later, the White Palace was finished.
When the fifth Dalai Lama departed this world in
    1682
news of his death was kept from everyone
while the sixth was secretly chosen and installed
with his minister, Sangay Gyatso, as regent.
He raised the Red Palace, story on top of story
just like the White Palace.
The 5th Dalai Lama had been dead for twelve
    years,
but since his death had been concealed
it was as if his mummy were still alive.

Lhasa

In Lhasa
all statues of Buddha appear to be sleeping.
Half of the monks are venerated beggars.
The people who revere the monks are themselves
    venerable,
their ears alive to each moment of a thousand
    years.
When the wind has had its fill of Lhasa,
it goes sweeping over the mountains.
The dust is the real spectacle.

Names

In the Himalayan world
ordinary peaks go unnoticed.
Only peaks of 7000 meters,
or 7500,
have been given one name or another.

Fine. Fine indeed.
This world grows radically new
so long as there remain far more peaks
without names
than with.

Do you have something to say?
Nothing.

Mount Sumeru

Mount Sumeru!
That mountain's a strong man's cock.
Phrases like "navel of the world"
or "crown of creation" fall short.
It's simply a cock.

A youth from south India,
on the far side of the Himalayas,
having heard tell of Mount Sumeru
again and again,
finally reached it
after twenty-seven years of trying.
By then he was an old man,
and it was simply a cock.

If so, he'd better hurry back home
and embrace the wife he left behind.
There's the navel of the world.
There's the crown of creation.
Let the gate open, let honey flow into the lotus.
That's a cock.

The Road to Chantse

Never do they recklessly lop branches
from poplars,
which they do not even think of as trees.
If someone ever dared use a poplar for firewood
he'd deserve whatever he got,
however severe the punishment
at the legendary hands of Shenrab Miwo
who could not help but descend
from the heights of Mount Kailas.

When it comes to the poplar,
twenty years or more must pass
before it is tenderly, thoughtfully felled
and used to build a two-stringed *erhu*
or a sacred chest.

Where a poplar has been cut down,
they plant a sapling on that spot.
The dead roots in the ground
will nourish the sapling's roots.
In June or July, a fresh young poplar will rise.

Anyone growing old is obliged to raise someone
    young.

Note: Shenrab Miwo is said to have founded the Bon
religion thirty thousand years ago.

Manasarovar Lake

That lake exists
as mother to ten thousand rivers.
In the rainy season
three hundred swans alight there together:
    splendid.
That's why it's bound to be the mother of all the
    rivers.
Mount Sumeru, the male,
looms in the distance.
The lake is filled to the brim with longing.
In it, always, the shadows of snowy peaks,
ever new.

Nettles

Nagarjuna in India
Wonhyo in Korea
Milarepa in Tibet.

While he was doing his penance
Milarepa ate nothing but boiled nettles day after
    day.
His whole body turned a pale nettle-green.

His one clay bowl, too,
by the end, had turned green.

Now that bowl, said Milarepa, has become my
    teacher.
Once the bowl is broken
I shall acknowledge
that everything in this world changes.

While he was murmuring those words,
the bowl broke and Milarepa disappeared.
Poor people, following him,
ate nettles for food and turned green too.

On the Way to the
Bon Monastery at Menri

I see no truth, only vanity.
As I move on across the northern slopes of the
    Himalayas
I am a traitor.

Ten years ago,
the reflections of the southern Himalayan peaks
floating below a lake in Nepal
were truth to me.
In a land on the equator in the Indian Ocean
where eighty per cent were illiterate,
the heat was truth to me.

Now it's not the same.
I've cast aside every kind of rapture,
every sort of devotion.

108 rooms,
in each a hundred thousand buddhas:
what's the use?

A traitor,
I deserve to be drawn and quartered.
The buddhas,
smash them all.

All in smithereens,
rain would fall,
multicolored.
The fluttering prayer-flags would be soaked.

The torrent below shouted out.
Grow weak and pray!
it shouted, raging madly.

To the Buddhism of Tibetans,
to all other sorts of Buddhism,
and all other faiths
I am a rebel and a traitor.

Tarchen

If I were like Rinpoche,
someone who has prayed for a long time,
someone who has long practiced Vispassana
    meditation,
what need would there be for words?

Observing silence,
day after day,
yet again day after day,
wouldn't make me tense. Not at all.

My master's heart brightly filled with light,
I too have no inward or outward being.

On one of those days of no talking,
from the far distance
with infinite slowness,
an old friend approaches.

A man with whom I once studied
in some previous life
approaches!

A so-called self
of unremittant, unspoken longing
stretched between heaven and earth,

that self of mine approaches.
Tarchen.

Note: Tarchen is the last village before Mt Kailash,
serving as base camp for the pilgrims. Its name derives
from the Sanskrit word Darshan, "sacred sight."

Mother

At last the great wall, 6350 kilometers long, came
    to an end.
It was on a street in Jiayuguan, a remote Chinese
    town,
one summer's day.
Every so often a naked beggar went walking by
carrying a flute.

We had no idea why we were heading for Lhasa.
Here
there are red, white, black desert sands;
there is nothing more to long for.

Late at night I was waiting for the sound of a flute,
hoping for something.
I waited,
and then in a dream
I saw my mother as she used to look.

That very day,
my mother who was ten thousand *li* away
set off for the world nine thousand *li* beyond.

Ah, Whiteness

Ah, whiteness!
Merciless whiteness of the Himalayan peaks!
I myself was loathsome.
All day
I longed for nightfall.

Even by night
I could not wipe away the whiteness
from within my heart.

I vomited.
Sticking a finger down my throat
I vomited up the remaining whiteness.

I wanted to join a gang.
I wanted to join a suicide squad.
Only later, when I came to love whiteness again,
were the forty peaks of the Himalayas anything
    other
than a gasping torment.

Doubts Concerning the Highlands

Surely, a true adult is someone above all
who never suddenly lashes out at a child.
Who simply nods as a child talks,
and replies in even tones
no matter how much the child,
even someone else's child, pesters him.

Tomorrow,
as the sun is drying the morning dew,
a lama will come to visit you.
Ask him
where your grandfather is now—
in what world.

I'm going on, further up,
to gather more yak's dung.

Save your questions for tomorrow.

Surely, a true adult
is someone who treats not only children but the
    world in that way
with the warm darkness of an evening rock that
    has not cooled off.

One Day

In the region of Ali I met one old man who would
    pee anywhere.
On his wrinkled face, no history of any kind.
As he walked along
he kept twisting and tugging some yak wool
with one hand inside his ragged clothes
and rolling the thread into a ball in the other.

Plaiting the woolen thread,
he produces a thicker string.

Such is a nomad's life.
When he erects his tent somewhere new,
he fastens it firmly with that thick string.
On leaving, days later, he packs up his belongings
    with it.

What is Manjushri's enlightening wisdom? Mere
    dust!

Note: Manjushri is the boddhisattva who embodies
the wisdom leading to enlightenment in Mahayana
Buddhism.

Evening Road

Blessed are they who still have somewhere to go.
My body, not yet fallen, walks on
almost invisibly,
invisibly,
toward the Himalayas,
onward
in the company of mirages.
The wind blows eastward.
It's been so long since I drank, amazed,
wine from a noctilucent cup,
It seems to be a thousand years ago
that I drank red wine
from a cup made of jade from Qilian Mountain.

There's no right place to pitch our tent,
so we go on and on.
Without lifting my head,
I cannot tell if there are stars in the sky,
or what's happening.

Dance

The moon had forgotten to set. They didn't have
    drums.
Past Dolma Pass,
5000 meters up, the ravine was covered with moss-
    grass.
There, nomads had pitched their tents
and gathered to sing and dance.

Far into the night
they were simply themselves.

The next morning
they were already taking down their tents.
They were bringing their five hundred sheep
to a distant watering-hole.
Though they had scarcely slept,
the day was as fresh as the sound of water.

After a night spent gasping in the thin air,
it was a new day for me, too.

A Five-Year-Old Child

A five-year-old,
he'd already begun to grow old.
He dug a cigarette butt out of the dirt,
re-rolled it and lit up.

He puffed out the smoke pretty well.
His mother left, driving black pigs.
My friend threw the child a pack of cigarettes.

The iron-hued, brown-hued mountains were
    endless, unchanging.
There were no trees.
I wanted to die.

The child was me in the next world.

Two-Humped Camel

Did you see the two-humped camels of Qinghai?
It would have been near Golmud,
which you must pass through
on the road to Lhasa.
Did you see the dust-rimmed eyes of a Bactrian
    camel
gazing blankly at the other side of the desert
some hundred *li* away
as if the closest of friends.

Its tongue bloody from chewing coarse camel-weed
but already on the mend,
the Bactrian was gazing across the desert with
    hungry eyes,
eyes oblivious to its long ages of hauling.
For what reason is the horizon at sunset so large
    and beautiful?

Given the sorrow that burdens this world,
have you stealthily loaded it between the camel's
    humps—
whatever is neither sorrow's *sore*
nor sorrow's *row*?
Humans are so much meaner than other animals.

With Never a Mirror

Washing with wind is fine.
Washing with sunshine is fine.
Body never washed
for a year, twelve or thirteen lunar months,
it's fine today just as it is.
Not even washed at birth,
a child just as it comes out is fine.
Growing up just as it grows up is fine.
Things like mirrors are useless.
Beneath the vast sky,
that mountain looking at me
and me looking at that mountain: just fine!

A Black-Eared Kite Today

The odor of Tibet has become mine..
Over there is Dhaulagiri peak,
more than half of it stripped of cloudcover.
Whatever cover remains seems from this distance
    to be mere cloud
but by now the whole mountain must be wrapped
    in heavy snowstorms.

The side facing me
is totally blank.

Sky hangs beyond sky.
Old black-eared kite, you alone
must be perennial:
in the midst of blue darkness,
a hole punched out in the sky.

Never in haste,
you flutter your wings
once, lightly,
and hang there;
just hang there.

Gazing, it would seem, without staring,
you see everything.
A young mouse's first outing,
the shade under rocks:
you look down so clearly.

$300,000 in Those Days

Long ago,
the birthplace of the Dalai Lama was under
 Chinese control.
In order for the little Dalai Lama to leave
and head for Lhasa,
he needed the permission of the Governor.

The Chinese Governor demanded a ransom:
 100,000,000 yuan.
The Potala Palace in Lhasa duly paid it.
Then he demanded another 300,000,000,
equivalent to $300,000 in those days.
With great difficulty, the palace administrators
managed to raise that huge sum and sent it off.

Only then could the little child
arrive in Lhasa as the 14th Dalai Lama
after a long journey lasting forty days.
The secrets of the Potala Palace
could not all be known
were he to spend a lifetime there.
He was afraid.
So afraid.

In Takster, the child's village,
the barley harvest failed.
Horses, cows and flocks of sheep died.

Taxes increased.
His sickly father
got up on the anniversary of the child's birth
and filled the butter lamp with oil.
The shade of the green plum tree was cool.
Such was the home he left.

One Night in Lhasa

On June 20, 1997,
six lamas were executed in a prison in Lhasa.
On that day in Dharamsala, India,
the Dalai Lama's goverment in exile
closed its doors,
suspending all activities.
The people there kept silence,
said nothing,
ate nothing.

July 5 was the Dalai Lama's birthday.
In the streets of Lhasa
I too received a baptism of flour,
white from head to foot.

That evening I looked up at the stars.
The stars' birthdays,
their memorial days.
My body was starlight through and through.

Solar Furnaces

The solar furnaces on the roof
of every house in Lhasa
lie on their backs, faces up to the sky.
Welcome.
Welcome.

The finest sunlight
should come down,
tempted and dazzled
by the coquetry of the furnaces.
Absorbing the sunlight
they grow ever warmer.

Ah, ecstatic climax;
lewd sounds are holy.
Warmer.
Warmer.

The furnaces grow hotter,
'til the water starts to boil.
Ah, ejaculation of despair.
Ohhh, and then prostration . . .
a cooling mouthful of butter-tea.

A Skull as a Drinking Cup

A master
offered a newly enlightened disciple
a cup of water.
The cup was a skull.

The master added:
Today is the last.
Accept a cup of wine.
The cup was a skull.

He brought out a rosary.
It was made from a skull.

I wish my skull too might become a drinking cup
some sad day in this world.

Auditory Hallucination

My friend's visit was most unexpected.
More a surprise, though, than a joy.

Only his voice had come.
I went outside barefooted
but he wasn't there.
The moon was brushing the roof.
It was the night after I'd visited Sera Monastery.
I'd taken off the glasses that had clung all day long
    to my face.

Already the Himalayas didn't entirely belong to the
    Earth.

Birthday

It was in Darchen, at the foot of Mount Kailas.
    There was so much shit.
Dried shit and not quite dried shit.
July 14, 1997, ten in the morning, my birthday.
I was not in my twenties but in my sixties.
Someone brought liquor.
Someone brought meat.
Young Tibetans hung scarves around my neck:
birthday wishes.

A three-legged dog with one front leg missing
came walking in from somewhere all by itself.

Darchen

Descending from an altitude of 6500 meters
to 4300 meters
I came back to life.
The breath in my breast grew warm and fluttering.
I longed for my wife.

Himalayan Cranes

On a high plateau to the north of the Himalayas
live small-bodied cranes.
They do little flying
and little eating.

The time had come.
They knew it better than anyone.

They fasted for several days,
grew ever lighter,
even slowed their breathing,
slow, slower.

Then, soaring into the sky like ghosts
they entered the air currents flowing above the
      peaks.
Lightly, lightly, they floated on.
Thus they passed over the Himalayas
and alit on the plains of Bihar in northern India.
That had been their home in past lives.
It was their home in the present.

Confession

I have something I want to say in secret.
In the Himalayas
there was nothing but the Himalayas.

Unless you put an end to yourself
somewhere in the Himalayas,
there was nothing to bring back

I was only too happy to leave there.
I suffered from dysentery so violent
that time itself spasmed, my now
at once five years past and five years hence.

Back down to 4000 meters, I felt like I'd arrived.
Reaching Lhasa at 3700 meters, I felt like I'd
     arrived.
The vertebra of my gaunt spine cracked in the air.
I fell into a deep sleep.

Leave-Taking

Looking closely into the mirror,
I longed to become something.
I have always been a mirror,
longing to become something
for the last thirty years.

I threw the mirror away, once and for all.
Smashcrash! Jjengkurang!
I was on my way back.

THE MARJORIE G. PERLOFF SERIES
OF INTERNATIONAL POETRY

This series is published in honor of Marjorie G. Perloff
and her contributions, past and present, to the literary
criticism of international poetry and poetics. Perloff's
writing and teaching have been illuminating and
broad-ranging, affecting even the publisher of
Green Integer; for without her influence and
friendship, he might never have engaged
in publishing poetry.

Selections from the Series

Yang Lian *Yi* (GI 35) [China]

Lyn Hejinian *My Life* (GI 39) [USA]

Hagiwara Sakutarō *Howling at the Moon* (GI 57)
[Japan]

Adonis *If Only the Sea Could Sleep* (GI 84)
[Syria/Lebanon]

Henrik Nordbrandt *The Hangman's Lament* (GI 95)
[Denmark]

André Breton *Earthlight* (GI 102) [France]

Paul Celan *Breathturn* (GI 111) [Bukovina/France]

Paul Celan *Threadsuns* (GI 112) [Bukovina/France]

Gilbert Sorrentino *New and Selected Poems* (GI 143)
[USA]

Ko Un *Ten Thousand Lives* (GI 123) [Korea]

Maurice Gilliams *The Bottle at Sea* (GI 124) [Belgium]

Visar Zhiti *The Condemned Apple* (GI 134) [Albania]

Paul Éluard *A Moral Lesson* (GI 144) [France]

Atilla József *A Transparent Lion* (GI 149) [Hungary]

Gonzalo Rojas *From the Lightning* (GI 155) [Chile]

Osip Mandelshtam *Tristia* (GI 156) [Russia]

Nishiwaki Junzaburō *A Modern Fable* (GI 157) [Japan]

Adriano Spatola *The Position of Things* (GI 165) [Italy]

Jean-Pierre Rosnay *When a Poet Sees a Chestnut Tree* (GI 166) [France]

Ko Un *Songs for Tomorrow* (GI 170) [Korea]

Tomas Tranströmer *The Sorrow Gondola* (GI 177) [Sweden]

Ko Un *Himalaya Poems* (GI 192) [Korea]

THE AMERICA AWARDS
for a lifetime contribution to international writing
Awarded by the Contemporary Arts Educational Project, Inc.
in loving memory of Anna Fahrni

The 2011 Award winner is:

KO UN [South Korea] 1933

Previous winners:
1994 Aimé Cesaire [Martinique] 1913–2008
1995 Harold Pinter [England] 1930–2008
1996 José Donoso [Chile] 1924-1996 (*awarded prior to his death*)
1997 Friederike Mayröcker [Austria] 1924
1998 Rafael Alberti [Spain] 1902-1999
1999 Jacques Roubaud [France] 1932
2000 Eudora Welty [USA] 1909-2001
2001 Inger Christensen [Denmark] 1935–2009
2002 Peter Handke [Austria] 1942
2003 Adonis (Ali Ahmad Said) [Syria/Lebanon] 1930
2004 José Saramago [Portugal] 1922-2010
2005 Andrea Zanzotto [Italy] 1921
2006 Julien Gracq (Louis Poirier) [France] 1910-2007
2007 Paavo Haavikko [Finland] 1931
2008 John Ashbery [USA] 1927
2009 Günter Kunert [GDR/Germany] 1929
2010 Javier Marías [Spain] 1951